CHRISTMAS & YOU

The Personality Connection

Pamela A. Taylor

Clear Lake, IA

Christmas & You:
The Personality Connection

2024 © Pamela A. Taylor
Cover & Interior Design by Heather Hart
Cover graphics © swkunst | Deposit Photos

TABLE OF CONTENTS

Before You Begin

Many of us enter this season of the year after a time of celebrating Thanksgiving to God for all we already have. For Thanksgiving—the main emphasis is on travel and food. Doing whatever it takes to share that yummy table together. And then the very next day is BLACK FRIDAY and we turn into TASK mode. Many rush to the stores or busy ourselves online to buy more things—All of that the very next day after we thanked God for all we already have. But it's a sale, so we believe we must go and buy and rush around. And so begins the season of frazzle. But...what if we CHOOSE to be different this year?

So, with that backdrop, let's CHOOSE to be more intentional with Christmas. We SAY Jesus is the reason for the season, but is He really? What if we actually ask ourselves "What DID Jesus do?" He totally understood each personality and He actually enjoyed each one He encountered. Let's do THAT this year!

That's what the first section of this Advent book is about. Embracing each other's differences. (To make it easy for you, we've made it possible to print off the lists so you can take it along with you as a type of "cheat sheet" to refer to as you go about your times together.) 😊

The second section of the book is a way to prepare your hearts spiritually for CHRISTmas with a devotion for each of the four weeks of advent. Each has a different focus to prepare your heart for the coming of the Christ Child. You might want to light an advent candle and read the devotion for the week together as a family. Or it would be great to do together with a Bible Study group. Or give it as an early Christmas gift for those who serve you...your mailman, your grocery clerk, your pharmacist, your neighbors, or for family or friends who won't be able to be with your physically. You can have a Skype call together lighting the candle, reading and praying.

Are you getting the idea? Let's DO what Jesus DID this year. Find ways to draw attention to the REASON we celebrate His birthday.

May your Merry Christmas be more of a MARY CHRISTMAS this year! Sitting at His feet. Blessing HIM by honoring others. I am praying for you! Let me know how it goes!

To God be the Glory!
God bless you bunches
KLU GIB

Personalities
& Christmas

Holidays Can Be a Challenge

Whether you celebrate holidays alone or with family, what has been your experience? Have you wished things could be different? Better?

Awareness of Your Feelings/Attitude is Crucial

As you think TOWARD the upcoming holiday, what are you feeling? What pressure are you experiencing? What do you fear? What do you hope for? What is your heart telling you?

Disappointments & Expectations

I know I used to dread holidays because I was often disappointed. I had expectations about how I wanted things to go and how I wanted people to act toward each other. Have you ever felt that way?

Do Any of These Words Describe the Mood of You or Others During Holidays?

Cranky
Inconvenienced

Cramped
Ungrateful
Grumpy
Tired
Overworked
Overwhelmed
Anxious
Disappointed
Discouraged

Choose Joy

God often reminds us that the CHOICE is ours to make…it's actually an attitude change. What if you decided to do what I have begun to do? By God's grace…To choose joy.

What if—like me—you prayerfully turn to your Father God and ask Him to help you choose a new way of handling holidays? Encouraging one another and choosing to listen and be kind to each other. Now that is true joy!

Changes are Freeing

What if, you begin to turn your cranksgiving attitude into times of gratitude for the small things…choosing an attitude of thanksgiving…choosing an attitude of gratitude for what is good and right and lovely in your world, rather than focusing on what is overwhelming you or hurting you.

"Rejoice always, pray without ceasing, in everything give thanks; for this is the will of God in Christ Jesus for you."
– I Thessalonians 5:16-18 (NKJV)

PERSONALITY TYPES AND CHRISTMAS GATHERINGS

We are each one hard-wired (how God made you). Learning to value the strengths of others makes everything better. THAT is God's plan for us humans.

So, here I am....Hoping to make Christmas better for you this year, I put together a mini list of a few of the personality differences. Maybe when you gather together, if you go forewarned and forearmed with a basic understanding of each, rather than trying to change each other. Rather than getting angry at each other for being WHO they ARE, it just might help the times when you are all together to be a bit more relaxed and enjoyable. That is my hope. My prayer.

I love studying the differences in people. We are an amazing bunch that God turned loose on the world. Let's do Him proud this Christmas by choosing to embrace each other's differences rather than fighting and squabbling.

We will learn who should be put in charge of task things and who should be in charge of people things. We will learn to give some longer to think things through and we will understand why some want everything decided NOW!

"To know your strengths is not boasting. The more we step into our God-given strengths, the more we will realize that God has given us everything to accomplish His purposes. When Moses questioned his God-given strengths in Exodus, 3 & 4, God replied, 'What is that in your hand?' Isn't it time you started living from your strengths and discover what God has placed in YOUR hand?"– *Personality & Jesus. Understand, Embrace, and Live Your God-Given Personality*

Don't settle for mediocrity. EMBRACE all that God created you to be. And learn to ENJOY all that others were created to be.

Here is a fun prompt to practice a bit before you get together.
(Study the personality types that follow; and then try to guess how they will each respond differently to this scenario.)

Liz the Lion

Task Person
Fast Paced
Quick to React
Short Fuse
Risk Taker
Aggressive

Response: Controlling

WHAT.
A Lion wants to know WHAT.
WHAT is the plan?
WHAT are we going to do to fix it QUICKLY?

Scenario:
It's a week before Christmas.
How prepared is Liz the Lion?
All the personality types are all different, remember.
Decorations, presents, baking, cleaning, oil change,
reservations, etc. The weather looks iffy.
What is Liz the Lion's reaction?
What if the trip is cancelled and
the gathering has to be cancelled?
How does she react?
So, NOW what?

Goldie the Golden Retriever

People Person
Slower Paced
Single Person Focused
NOT Driven by Emotions

Response: Resists Change

HOW.
A Golden Retriever wants to know HOW.
HOW do you want me to do this?
HOW can I please you?

Scenario:
It's a week before Christmas.
How prepared is Goldie the Golden Retriever?
Decorations, presents, baking, cleaning, oil change,
reservations, etc. The weather looks iffy.
What is Goldie the Golden Retriever's reaction?
What if the trip is cancelled and
the gathering has to be cancelled?
How does she react?
So, NOW what?

Olivia the Otter

People Person
Fast Paced
Optimistic
Outgoing
Accepting

Response: People Pleaser

WHO.
An otter wants to know WHO.
WHO will be there?
WHO can I impress or influence?

Scenario:

It's a week before Christmas.
How prepared is Olivia the Otter?
Decorations, presents, baking, cleaning, oil change,
reservations, etc. The weather looks iffy.
What is Olivia the Otter's reaction?
What if the trip is cancelled and
the gathering has to be cancelled?
How does she react?
So, NOW what?

Betty the Beaver

Task Person
Slower Paced
Cautious
Low-Risk-Taker
Complies with Rules
Conservative

Response: Judgmental

WHY.
A Beaver wants to know WHY
WHY are we doing this?

Scenario:
It's a week before Christmas.
How prepared is Betty the Beaver?
They are all different, remember.
Decorations, presents, baking, cleaning, oil change,
reservations, etc. The weather looks iffy.
What is Betty the Beaver's reaction?
What if the trip is cancelled and
the gathering has to be cancelled?
How does she react?
So, NOW what?

GET YOUR CHEAT SHEET

Understand why those around you are the way they are and why they do the things they do this Christmas.

Get your Christmas Cheat Sheet:
PamelaATaylor.com/free-christmas-cheat-sheet/

Take the Assessment

Visit MinistryInsights.com to take the
Leading from Your Strengths personality assessment and
start Living from Your Strengths today!

This is not a test. There's no right or wrong answers.
Be honest and trust your first response. Don't second
guess yourself.

Use the coupon code: PAMTAYLOR
to get 15% off your purchase

Advent
Devotions

ADVENT WEEK ONE
A Christmas Prayer. Hope

As we celebrate the birthday of our Lord Jesus Christ, I pray the focus this year will in all ways be on the "reason for the season". Jesus. And that the light of His love brings you hope, salvation, peace, wisdom, and joy!

> "Therefore God also has highly exalted Him and given Him the Name which is above every name, that at the Name of Jesus every knee shall bow..."
> Philippians 2:9-10

Dictionary Definition of Advent
A period of getting ready for the coming of something or someone that is important or worthy of note. The period begins four Sundays before Christmas. It is observed by some with a period of prayer and fasting. Synonyms of Advent are: appear, coming, arrival. incoming.

C S Lewis
"Once in our world, a stable had something in it that was bigger than our whole world."

Christmas Rush vs. Christmas Hush

Many of us enter this season after a time of celebrating Thanksgiving to God for all we already have. We have tasks to accomplish, but the main emphasis is on people. Being together. Enjoying one another. Sharing a table together. And then the very next day is BLACK FRIDAY and we turn into TASK mode. Many rush to the stores or online to buy more things—the very next day after we thanked God for all we have. But it's a sale, so we must go and buy and rush around and begin the season of frazzle. I am reminded of the Veggie Tales movie "Stuff Mart". If you haven't seen it, you might want to add that to your list of Family Video Night choices.

What if this year could be different?

We always say this year will be different, but then we fall into old habits. Let's plan to CHOOSE to be different this year. Let's start now, with week One of Advent.

Advent Week One. Prophesy. Jesus. Hope.

"For unto us a child is born; unto us a son is given; and the government shall be upon his shoulder. These will be his royal titles: Wonderful. Counselor. The Mighty God. The Everlasting Father. The Prince of Peace."

Isaiah 9:6

John Piper

"I am prone to be dull, spiritually drowsy, halfhearted, lukewarm. That is the way human beings are, including Christians, even about great things. Peter knows it and is writing to awaken or to stir up his readers so that they don't just know but also feel the wonder of the truth."

POWERFUL!

Let's get "stirred up" this year.

Let's be radical for Jesus. Where is our HOPE? In stuff and gifts and parties and running ourselves ragged? Let's wake from our slumber. Spiritual drowsiness, BE GONE!!! Peter's aim was to remind us and then to stir us up. Waking us from our slumber. He says…

> "I think it right, as long as I am in this body,
> to stir you up by way of reminder."
>
> 2 Peter: 1:13

> "I am stirring up your sincere mind by way of reminder."
>
> 2 Peter 3:1

Let's DO this! Because the alternative is sad.

A Christmas Prayer

Hope arrived on that day. Pray with me…

Father, thank you for this opportunity to re-calibrate each year. To remember that Christmas is celebrating PROPHESY fulfilled with the arrival of HOPE. Will we allow our emotions and affections for the Savior to be stirred up as we are awaiting Christmas Day, remembering the greatest wonder of all? With your help and sweet reminders, Father God, we will make this year different. Better. We choose to anticipate the reminder of the arrival of the person of Jesus Christ, the Son of God, the Savior, to this world.

Will you choose Christmas Rush or Christmas Hush this year? Will you post the reminder on your refrigerator?

This Week's Verse

> "May the God of hope fill you with all joy and peace as you trust in him, so that you may overflow with hope by the power of the Holy Spirit."
>
> Romans 15:13

ADVENT WEEK TWO
Mary and Joseph. Obedience

Sometimes I think there is too much "ME" in me. Do you ever feel that way? Especially at Christmas–when we want so much to be Jesus-centered–we can tend to get ME centered. Overwhelmed. Weary. Busy. Distracted. Bossy. And likely focusing on how everything affects ME personally? Too busy to sit and just BE with our Lord, pondering the significance of all that transpired around His birth. Think of it, God came down. From Heaven. From royalty, to a human birth experience. Powerful! A deep and stunning love that knows no bounds!

I am right at this moment sitting in a temptation to condemn myself. What about you? My love is so often conditional. And I get busy with tasks. And a bit grumpy. This is all proof that I have not even BEGUN to grasp the details of what my Savior experienced to PROVE His love for me. For you. So, I am so grateful that...

"There is therefore now no condemnation to them which are in Christ Jesus, who walk not after the flesh, but after the Spirit."

Romans 8:1

Mary and Joseph

Yes, sadly, there is too much ME in me. And I have a feeling you are right there with me on this! But... astoundingly, Mary and Joseph were NOT full of themselves. There was NOT too much ME in them. Think of all they must have experienced. Gossip. Criticism. Fear. The vast unknown. They never waivered. The angel spoke and they believed and obeyed. NO ONE had EVER walked that path before. And NO ONE has walked it since then, either!

They Knew the Scriptures

Evidently —in view of their responses to their angel visits—they both knew the Scriptures well. What do you think you would have done? Have YOU ever had an encounter with an angel? Would you believe and obey like they did?

Mary Believed

When the angel said she would bear the Christ child, her only question was "HOW? How was that even possible, since she was a virgin?"

Joseph believed the angel that Mary was NOT unfaithful to him, but rather had been CHOSEN to be the virgin mother of the Lord. Joseph did not question. These were amazing young people! Even with their pure faith, it must have been difficult living in their community. Do you think other girls were jealous of her? Or do you think maybe no one even believed their story? Put yourself into the story and IMAGINE what it was like. They were real people.

"Now the birth of Jesus Christ was as follows: 'After His mother Mary was betrothed to Joseph, before they came together, she was found with Child of the Holy Spirit."
Matthew 1:18 (NKJV)

Who are Mary and Joseph?

Are we doing a disservice by only making Christmas about a sweet baby in the manger, in a clean stable, surrounded by nice clean animals and shepherds worshiping the newborn baby? I think of a favorite book, also made into a movie "The Best Christmas Pageant Ever". Every year I read the children's book and watch the movie. It reminds me how we get it all wrong even performing the Christmas pageant. Pageant preparations and practices are often full of tension. Every mother wants her daughter to play the part of Mary and no one wants to be the angels. Each one wants to have a MAIN CHARACTER part. We portray it as "romantic" and lovely and sweet, when it was anything BUT that! It was difficult in every sense of the word.

They were a poor couple, likely experiencing scorn in their community. Then, leaving their family and all that was familiar, they went to an UNfamiliar place. Giving birth in a smelly barn. No running water. No central heat. No family to give comfort and support. No medication to dull the pain of delivery.

Our Savior came TO us. From Heaven. Mary and Joseph sacrificed all their dreams of what we call a "normal" life.

"But while he thought about these things, behold, an angel of the Lord appeared to him in a dream, saying, 'Joseph, son of David, do not be afraid to take you Mary, your wife, for that which is conceived in her is of the Holy Spirit' She will give birth to a son, and you are to give him the name Jesus, because he will save his people from their sins"
                                                            Matthew 1:20-21

Week Two. Obedience. Bethlehem

The angel quotes from Isaiah 7:14 to Joseph–that the baby will be named Jesus. Immanuel. God with us. Joseph believed the angel and married Mary immediately. And they obeyed and named the baby Jesus.

Two young people followed their call. Through their obedience, the way was prepared for Christ to bless us. The day Jesus was born was the day Immanuel happened. He is most definitely God with us. Do you believe that? I hope you do.

Why DID Christmas happen?

"You know that He appeared in order to take away sins, and in Him there is no sin…the reason the Son of God appeared was to destroy the works of the devil."

I John 2:5, 8

"…being fully persuaded (assured) that what He had promised, He was able also to perform."

Romans 4:21

Evangelist Vance Havner
"We are to do more than just be ready. We are to be expectant."

John Piper
"Eternity waits for our response. Don't lose this opportunity to make Christmas different this year. How sad if Christmas is just another busy time of year, and we miss the "REASON FOR THE SEASON". May the Spirit of God use these words to open your eyes afresh to the glories of Christ and give you a new taste of your indestructible joy."

Immanuel arrived that day. Pray with me.
Father, give us the attitude of expectancy. Don't let this be an ordinary Christmas. Help us to seek you differently this year. Better. Focused. Thank you for this opportunity to reevaluate the way we enter into this Christmas season. May we look at Christmas through fresh eyes. To remember that Christmas is about OBEDIENCE. Being called to a higher ground of faith and trust in You, our Creator God. You sacrificed so much Yourself, Father. You allowed Your Son

to suffer through living as a human person, with all the suffering and sorrow and even joy that brings.

Lord Jesus, help us to step up into the responsibilities we have each day with obedience and joy. And to keep a proper perspective. This world is not our home. We are only passing through. Bless the work of our hands and bless others through us.

Holy Spirit, in those places where we can represent our Jesus, our Savior, speak to us and give us wisdom. Speak through us so that others will be drawn to Him. Immanuel. God with us. Just like you did for Mary and Joseph, Father. May we, too, be as trusting and obedient. Give us a hunger for Your Word. And for a personal relationship with You.

This Week's Verse

"The life I now live in the flesh I live by faith in the Son of God, who loved me and gave Himself for me."

Galatians 2:20

ADVENT WEEK THREE
The Shepherds. Joy

Have you ever felt like you didn't matter? Unloved. Ignored. Like an outcast? I know I have. You are not alone in that. Many are lost. Many are full of anxiety and fear. Do you think that is how the shepherds in the Christmas story felt?

I don't know about you, but I need to continually "reboot" my "brain" to "refresh" from what I see and hear day-to-day. The theme this third week of Advent is the Shepherds' response of Joy. David Jeremiah said: "We are so used to Christmas that we have become dazed by the season, rather than amazed by the REASON." The shepherds were not dazed. They were most definitely amazed!

These are precious stories of real people in the Bible. They all point us to pieces of the puzzle in the Jesus story. This Christmas season, let's help make the Bible come alive for those in our orbit. Will we CHOOSE to be alert for those who feel ignored? Maybe there is someone who needs to find their way back into the fold. Jesus is The GOOD Shepherd. If you have welcomed Him into your life as Savior and Lord, then He is YOUR Shepherd. In the Scriptures, Jesus is also called The Lamb of God. He willingly sacrificed Himself. If you have decided to follow Him as your Savior, then He has become your very own personal sacrificial Lamb.

Have you ever felt like you didn't matter?

The Shepherds in the Christmas Story

Our focus—on this third week of advent—is the lonely shepherds on the hillside, caring for the sheep for the temple sacrifices. These shepherds were despised. Uneducated. They were outcasts because of their necessary isolation from religious ordinances and observances. They were dirty and considered spiritually unclean. Unable to enter the Temple to worship on any of the holy days because they were so busy doing the dirty, under-appreciated work on the hillside with the stubborn, sometimes dumb sheep. These outcasts were the exact ones CHOSEN by GOD to be the very first to receive the message that the SAVIOR was born in Bethlehem. Isn't that just like our God? He often does the opposite of what we might expect.

The Shepherds' Duties

It was a physically demanding job. They were continually outdoors in extremes of heat and cold. Perhaps they are wearing coarse woolen coats made from sheep's wool. Outcasts—yet, they were a vital part of the Jewish economy. They made possible the "temporal" sacrifices in the temple, as all awaited the day of the coming of the "permanent" sacrifice (Jesus). At night, they built a fence around the sheep, and protected the entrance from predators. They made sure the sheep were safe. The sheep knew, recognized, and obeyed the shepherd's voice.

The shepherd knew each one individually. These amazing men have literally given up their NORMAL way of life—FOR THE SHEEP. They have sacrificed a NORMAL life in order to serve the greater community. They loved their work. These shepherds were caring for and providing the sacrifices for the sins of the people. So, it is no surprise that when the angels appeared to announce the news of the Savior's birth, they were already alert to anything unusual.

"...there were shepherds living out in the fields, keeping watch over their flock by night. And behold, an angel of the Lord stood before them, and the glory of the Lord shone around them, and they were greatly afraid. Then the angel said to them, "Do not be afraid, for behold, I bring you good tidings of great joy which will be to all people. For there is born to you this day in the city of David, a Savior, who is Christ the Lord. And this will be a sign to you. You will see a babe wrapped in swaddling cloths, lying in a manger. And suddenly there was with the angel a multitude of the heavenly host praising God..."

Luke 2:8-13

They Believed

They had no doubts. They were initially afraid. (Lots of bright lights in the middle of the night tend to do that to a person!) But when they heard the angel's news, they believed it!

They didn't argue with each other or try to explain it away. They simply believed. (That is what the Lord asks of us, as well. When He "appears" to us in any way, He expects us to believe and obey like these lowly outcast shepherds.)

The "World" Doesn't Understand

Have you ever felt like you didn't matter? – Your faith can make a difference!

If you are a fully devoted follower of Jesus, then undoubtedly, there have been times in your life when people thought you were a bit too "religious" or maybe even "wacko".

"Christ is worth infinitely more than what we see, touch, or gain in this quick and temporal life. He is worth leaving houses, lands, and loved ones. He is worth selling everything for. He is worth the often-humiliating wait at the back of the world's line. The world will look at you with ridicule for whatever it is you gave up for Christ (like the shepherds in Biblical times). BUT, the world won't see that, in Him, you now stand at the front of the line. Jesus changes everything!"

Anchor Devotional

"Heaven will be full of those of whom the world is not worthy. Rejoice to be in that group!" (See Hebrews 11:38)

They acted without delay.

When the angels had gone from them back to heaven, they said to each other, "Let's go!" They believed and acted on that "which the Lord has made known to us." The Scriptures say that they went "with haste" and that they saw it was true. Sure enough, there was Mary and Joseph and the baby in the manger just as they were told. THEN, what did they do?

They JOYFULLY told everybody.

"Now when they had seen Him, they made widely known the saying which was told them concerning the child."
John 2:17

And the people marveled about what they were told by the shepherds. Remember. These are introverts. They are smelly. They are not used to being in town or around a bunch of people. They are most comfortable with each other and with the sheep. They are unschooled. Outcasts. Yet, they forget about the fact that they were nobodies. They knew in their "KNOWER" that it was true! They had no doubt. No one could talk them out of what they had personally experienced.

They did not hold back. They were totally in awe and wanted everyone to know. That's what happens when you meet the Lord personally. You cannot hold back the Good News. What about you? Are you in the before or after state of what the shepherds experienced? Do you know Him personally? What about those you do life with? Do they know your story about when YOU met Jesus? (When you discovered personally that Jesus is who He says He is.)

David Jeremiah asked in his devotional:

"Will you share the true Christmas message this year with those who need to hear about God's love and forgiveness?"

Back to the shepherds…After all this, what did they do?

They returned to their work.

The Lord tells us to "occupy" until He comes (again). We are not to go and hide until He comes back for us. We are to go about out daily duties, BUT always with one eye towards Heaven, WAITING with EXPECTANCY for Him to appear with a shout!

Joy arrived that day. Pray with me.

Holy God, thank You for the story of these shepherds who actually witnessed what the angel had told them. It was/is true. And they were jumping for joy. They would never again think of themselves as despised outcasts. They knew they had witnessed that "Heaven came down" that Christmas day. I pray for Your strength today to think clearly, serve creatively, and follow you consistently. Father, You have all authority in Heaven and on earth. Fill my mind with clear convictions that You are in charge. Empower me to stand true to You! Give me an unassuming servant heart like the shepherds. I know that You never ask me to do anything more than You will provide the strength to accomplish. I am so grateful for this season of the year. Thank You, Jesus. You left your palatial home to come down to live with Your creation and show us the way

HOME. Never ever let me take that for granted. Never let me take YOU for granted. YOU are AMAZING! Glory, glory, glory! You deserve all Glory, honor, praise and thanksgiving. I want to be a JOY GERM…infecting as many people as possible each day…drawing them to YOU, the reason for our joy!

This Week's Verse

"Then, the shepherds returned, glorifying and praising God for all the things that they had heard and seen, as it was told them."

Luke 2:20

ADVENT WEEK FOUR
The King Is Coming. Love

I'd like to start week four with a blessing for each of you: May you have a "Mary" Christmas with many opportunities to just sit and allow yourself to enter into a time of WONDER, worship, and praise for the Reason (Jesus) for the Season. Just for fun, let's have a minute of sharing some potential family/friend gathering conversation starters. Some fun eye-openers you might not know...

Things We Believe...However...
- The angels did NOT "sing"
- There is no mention of an INN KEEPER
- The wise men were NOT at the "stable" where the "babe" was
- There is no mention of a DONKEY for Mary to ride on
- Jesus was NOT a "baby" when the wise men arrived at the "house"
- There is no mention of the number of wise men

Now...let's look at the next chapter of our advent story of Christmas...

Worth the Trip

> "Now after Jesus was born in Bethlehem of Judea in the days of Herod the king, behold, wise men from the East came to Jerusalem, saying, 'Where is He who has been born King of the Jews? For we have seen His star in the East and have come to worship Him.'
>
> Matthew 2:1

The wise men probably traveled hundreds of miles over many months, in order to honor the newborn king with their treasures. These expensive and unusual gifts suggest they were official representatives sent as emissaries to honor the new king of this ancient land. And they probably had some form of body-guards because of the value of the gifts. They never took their eyes off the star. They stayed on course because they believed the extraordinary star they had never seen before, would lead them to an extraordinary person. They came to give their gifts to He who IS the GIFT.

The Visual Guide to Bible Events suggests that perhaps they were descendants of those sent east during the Babylonian captivity in the days of Daniel, and had returned to their homeland seeking the Messiah.

These "wise" men, knew prophesy. They were philosophers, priests, scholars. Perhaps they had spent their entire lives looking for the star to guide them.

> "A star will come out of Jacob;
> a scepter will rise out of Israel."
>
> Numbers 24:17

Herod the Great

He knew he did not deserve his title of king. He was power hungry and fearful of losing his power – dubbed as King by the Roman Senate as King of the Jews. He had even killed his sons and wives when he felt they were conspiring to overtake his throne. His royal paranoia was deeply intact when the Magi arrived. Imagine how he felt when he heard that the Magi were looking for the LEGITIMATE King of the Jews. He pumped the Magi for information pretending that he, too, wanted to go to worship Him whom they sought. The one whom Scripture had prophesied.

So, when Herod learned that his RIVAL was a child, likely 2 years old, and lived in Bethlehem, he sent his murderous soldiers to kill ALL male children 2 years old and younger. Imagine the uproar in the town. There were two groups. One brought gifts and the other brought terror:

** The magi (Matthew Henry's Commentary on the Bible suggests there could have been up to 14 magi, along with their body guards) and

** The soldiers (and who knows how many of them there were). The town was chaotic and overrun with strangers.

Background (Source: Matthew Henry's Commentary of the Bible)

In Moses' time, Pharaoh ordered male Jewish children murdered at birth, just before the Exodus FROM Egypt TO the Promised Land (The exile).

Now, Herod orders the slaughter of Israelite children IN the promised land. This sends Joseph and family BACK TO Egypt to safety. (It was the closest place outside of Herod's jurisdiction, and there were thriving Jewish communities there, which offered Joseph and family a safe haven.)

God speaks to each of us uniquely.

At the birth of Christ, God notified the JEWISH shepherds by an angel.

At the birth of Christ, God notified the GENTILE magi (wise men) with a star.

He spoke in their own language—in the way they were best acquainted with.

How does God speak to YOU when He wants to get YOUR attention?

Tiring Journeys. Worth the Trip

Mary and Joseph had traveled maybe 90 miles to Bethlehem because of the census.

The wise men had traveled maybe thousands of miles on their long journey that must have lasted a couple years, because of Jesus.

God will provide for you, too. For every mile of your "journey" with Him. He will give you whatever you need. Not what you THINK you need, but what you actually need in order to complete what He has called you to do.

Christmas

According to Mark 10:45 Christmas is about the coming of the Son of Man who "came not to be served but to serve, and give his life as a ransom for many."

John Piper

"These words ...are what I hope God will fix in your mind and your heart this Advent. Open your heart to receive the best present imaginable: Jesus giving himself to die for you and to serve you all the rest of eternity. Receive this. Turn away from self-help and sin. Become like little children. Trust him TRUST HIM. with your life."

Love arrived that day. Pray with me.

May God fill you with a sense of WONDER this Christmas season and beyond. May you search for Him everywhere, every day, in every way. Because He is right there with you, through it all. Believe that! WHATEVER you are experiencing. He is the way, the Truth and the Life. I pray you have more of a MARY Christmas than a MERRY Christmas this year.

Lord, give us wisdom to follow the "star" You have for each of us to follow. Show us the way. We thank you for giving us Your Spirit, so we can think Your thoughts as we gather with others. And as we sit alone with You—thinking through our day each evening. Asking how we can bless You more tomorrow...to bring You joy. You ARE Love. May Your Wisdom and the Light of Your Love shine through each one of us, no matter what! Thank You Jesus for your sacrifice...to show us the way HOME. May we CHOOSE to love You with an undivided heart. To God be the Glory!

This Week's Verse:

"Now to Him who is able to keep you from stumbling, and to present you faultless before the presence of His glory with exceeding joy, to God our Savior, who alone is wise, be glory and majesty, dominion and power, both now and forever. Amen.

Jude 24-25

FINALE

I believe in God. But, what is amazing is that God believes in me! Do you have that kind of relationship with Him? I sure hope so!

Just think about it...

How is it possible that the God who created the universe and everything in it, including you and me, wants to have a close relationship with His creation—you and me? He desires to be our first thought in the morning and our last thought when we go off to sleep each night. He wants to be a part of everything that matters to you. To be your best Friend. He loves it when you just sit and chat with Him about your day. And when you ask Him to give you His wisdom about a situation.

Do you WANT that?

Or are you content being just an earth dweller, living day-to-day with no thought of eternity? Be honest with yourself. We can embrace the relationship. Or we can push Him away, but that makes Him sad.

What do you actually think about Jesus?

Who is He to you? The baby in the manger? The man on the cross? He is both. And so much more.

Laurie Beth Jones tells a story:

A man was talking with a woman who knew she was dying very soon. "What does it feel like to live each day knowing you are dying?"

The woman's response surprised him. "What does it feel like living each day PRETENDING that you are not?"

My Dad had a saying

"It's time to take stock of yourself." Would you live your life differently, if you were told you have 6 months to live? So, where are you with the Lord? Distant? Close? Lukewarm? Are you a maybe-later type of person? How are you living now? And is there anything you'd change in order to live your life with your eyes on Heaven as your true home? Do you KNOW Him? REALLY know Him? As Savior AND Lord? As the terminally ill lady asked the curious man: Are you PRETENDING the end is not near?

Is the Lord returning soon?

Pastor Jeremiah asks: Are you Rapture Ready? Pastors David Jeremiah, Jentezen Franklin, and John Hagee this very month (October 2023) are all three preaching and teaching about prophesy and the rapture. They all believe the time is near and nothing else on the prophetic calendar has to be fulfilled before the Rapture happens. And, with the war in Israel happening right now, and the prophesies that are already fulfilled, it leads us to believe the prophesies yet to be. We see disease, wars, and rumors of wars. We are still harming and killing our dear children. Our own US border is not secure, with no information WHO are pouring in illegally. Are these the signs of the times the Bible warns about?

Your response

You probably are not going to say: "I'm going to sell everything and give all my possessions to the poor." God tells us to "occupy" (work) until He comes (again). But, will your response be to change your companions, or change how you spend your free time? Or what about your thought life and your words? How do you spend your money? Does the Lord get your first fruits? Are you spending more and more time in the "instruction manual" (the Bible)?

What if you honor the Lord with your life?

God doesn't want lukewarm or cold followers. Rather, God calls us to be a Fully Devoted Follower of Jesus. Each of us is imperfect, but are we progressively becoming more intimately acquainted with Him and the wonders of His person...choosing to follow and learn more about Him and seek Him in all things? What has He called you be? To do?

ALWAYS with your eye on Heaven

It has been said that when we live with an eye toward Heaven, sin becomes unattractive. We must diligently cultivate a love for Him that is so great that the lust of the flesh, the lust of the eyes, and the boastful pride of life cannot get in the door of our heart.

Dear friend, are you PRETENDING you have a lot of time to first have fun before you decide? How would you live your life today if you knew for certain that Jesus was coming for you this week either through death or the Rapture? Would you do anything differently? Jesus loves you so very, very much, He even died for you, so you can be with Him forever in Heaven. He hates being separated from you. However, No one comes to God-the-Father's House, except through deliberately deciding to be a Christ follower. God has no grandchildren. It is a very personal choice. And that choice is yours to make. He will not force it on you, but if you say no, or "wait", it breaks His heart!

Perhaps today

Let's live today and every day as if it is so: Perhaps Today! Because it COULD be so!

Often, when people came to Jesus for help, He would ask: *"What do you want Me to do for you?"* How will you answer that question today?

Be ready because if He comes today, there will no longer be time to GET ready.

Merry Christmas
>Awaiting His shout,
>Pam Taylor

Got a Minute?

If this book has impacted your life, please take a moment to let someone know.

Here are a few ways you can show your support:
- Write a book review.
- Share or mention *Christmas & You* on social media.
  Be sure to use the hashtag #LFYS.
- Recommend this book to your friends, family, Bible study sisters, church family, or anyone else you think might enjoy it as much as you have.
- Check out the other books in the Living From Your Strengths Trilogy.
- Visit me online at PamelaATaylor.com.

About the Author

Pam Taylor is passionately in love with Jesus Christ and delights in walking with Him daily. Her greatest joy has been providing for and raising her "now" two adult children. As a result of being a single, homeschooling mom and former missionary to third world countries, Pam discovered her gifts for teaching, discipling, and writing.

You can learn more about Pam and connect with her online at PamelaATaylor.com

THE LIVING FROM
YOUR STRENGTHS TRILOGY

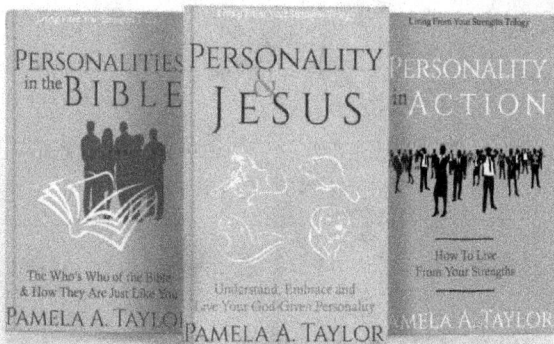

Visit Pam online to find all the books
in the Living from Your Strengths Trilogy.

www.ingramcontent.com/pod-product-compliance
Lightning Source LLC
Chambersburg PA
CBHW060646280326
41933CB00012B/2173